TODAY'S SUPERSTARS Sports

Rafael NADAL

by Geoffrey M. Horn

GARETH**STEVENS**
GS
PUBLISHING
A Member of the WRC Media Family of Companies

Please visit our web site at: **www.garethstevens.com**
For a free color catalog describing Gareth Stevens Publishing's
list of high-quality books and multimedia programs, call
1-800-542-2595 (USA) or 1-800-387-3178 (Canada).
Gareth Stevens Publishing's fax: (877) 542-2596.

Library of Congress Cataloging-in-Publication Data

Horn, Geoffrey M.
    Rafael Nadal / by Geoffrey M. Horn.
      p. cm. — (Today's superstars: sports)
    Includes bibliographical references and index.
    ISBN-10: 0-8368-6184-1   ISBN-13: 978-0-8368-6184-6 (lib. bdg.)
    1. Nadal, Rafael, 1986- 2. Tennis players—Spain—Biography—
Juvenile literature. I. Title.
GV994.N37H67   2006
796.342092—dc22   2005028961

This edition first published in 2006 by
Gareth Stevens Publishing
A Weekly Reader® Company
1 Reader's Digest Rd.
Pleasantville, NY 10570-7000 USA

This edition copyright © 2006 by Gareth Stevens, Inc.

Editor: Jim Mezzanotte
Art direction and design: Tammy West
Picture research: Diane Laska-Swanke

Photo credits: Cover, © Nick Laham/Getty Images; pp. 5, 7, 11, 14
© AP/Wide World Photos; pp. 13, 23, 25 © Matthew Stockman/
Getty Images; p. 17 © Julian Finney/Getty Images; p. 18 © Christophe
Simon/AFP/Getty Images; p. 21 © Clive Brunskill/Getty Images;
p. 26 © Timothy A. Clary/AFP/Getty Images, p. 28 © Pierre-Philippe
Marcou/AFP/Getty Images

Printed in the United States of America

2 3 4 5 6 7 8 9 10 09 08 07

CONTENTS

CHAPTER 1

KING OF CLAY

In the first half of 2005, a teenager from Spain turned the tennis world upside down. His name is Rafael Nadal, but fans in his native country know him as Rafa. How hot is Rafa? When he won the French Open in June 2005, the King and Queen of Spain came to the stadium to cheer him on. Today, he attracts fans wherever he goes.

Open Season

In December 2004, Nadal was ranked fifty-first on the men's pro tour. By July 2005, he was ranked second. The key to his rapid rise was his stunning win at the French

FACT FILE

Nadal's last name is pronounced nah-DAHL. His nickname, Rafa, is pronounced RAH-fah. He is 6 feet, 1 inch (1.9 meters) tall. His official weight is 188 pounds (85 kilograms).

The Grand Slam

The four biggest tennis tournaments held each year are called the Grand Slam. Each Grand Slam event is played outdoors.

First comes the Australian Open. It is played on hard courts and usually takes place in January. The next Grand Slam tournament is the French Open. It begins in late May in Paris, France. The French Open is the only Grand Slam event played on clay.

The third Grand Slam event is Wimbledon. This tournament is played in England in late June and early July. Wimbledon is the only Grand Slam event played on grass. The final Grand Slam event held each year is the U.S. Open. This tournament is held at the National Tennis Center in New York City. The U.S. Open is played on hard courts. It takes place in late August and early September.

Rafa's exciting play thrilled fans as he beat Mariano Puerta in the French Open final.

Open. It is one of four Grand Slam events, which are the biggest tennis tournaments played each year.

The French Open is held at Roland Garros Stadium in Paris. At this stadium, the courts are red clay. Clay courts are slower than grass or hard courts. The ball bounces higher, giving the players more time to get ready for the next shot. Serves are easier to return. Rallies — the times when players keep hitting the ball back and forth to each other — are longer. You need to play great defense and have tremendous stamina to be a world-class clay court champion.

Nadal's skills are perfect for clay. He has been playing on red clay courts since he was a young boy. Rafa works hard for every point. He races from one side of the court to the other. He returns balls that many players wouldn't even try to

FACT FILE

One of Rafa's most powerful weapons is the heavy topspin he often puts on the ball. His racket brushes the back of the ball with a sharp upward stroke. The ball flies hard, high, and deep, and it bounces high. It is a tough shot to return.

hit. He slides, lunges, and dives to make tough shots. At the end of a hard match on a clay court, Rafa's clothes are dirty with red dust.

Grand Slam Win

Rafa missed the French Open in 2003 because of an elbow injury. A bad ankle kept him out of the French Open in 2004. But nothing could stop Rafa in 2005 — not even the number-one player, Roger Federer.

To get to the final, Nadal had to beat Federer in the semifinal match. The match

Federer and Nadal greet each other after their semifinal match at Roland Garros Stadium.

was played on June 3 — Rafa's nineteenth birthday. He celebrated by taking Federer in four sets, 6-3, 4-6, 6-4, 6-3. Federer, who made sixty-two unforced errors, explained his loss by saying that he had "started bad and finished bad."

Nadal was a heavy favorite in the final against Mariano Puerta of Argentina. He stumbled in the first set, losing in a tiebreak. He had an easier time in the next two sets. A 7-5 victory in the hard-fought fourth set gave him the championship.

The left-hander's win in Paris made history in more ways than one. He was the first player since 1982 to win the French Open on his first try. He was also the first teenager to win a Grand Slam event since Pete Sampras in 1990. Rafa's victory marked his twenty-fourth straight match win, breaking the record for a teenager set in 1988 by Andre Agassi.

FACT FILE

By winning the French Open in 2005, Nadal earned more than $1 million.

Tennis by the Numbers

Rafa won his French Open final match against Mariano Puerta by a score of 6-7(6), 6-3, 6-1, 7-5. But what do these numbers mean?

In Grand Slam men's singles, a player wins a match by taking three sets out of five. Each set must include at least six games. The players take turns serving, with each player serving for a whole game. The first player to win six games usually wins the set. Nadal's 6-3 score in the second set means that he won six games while Puerta won only three.

What about that 7-5 score in the final set? Here's where the scoring gets more complicated. If a set is tied at five games apiece, the winner must win by two games. The 7-5 margin means that after the score was tied at five, Nadal took the last two games to win the set and the match.

In the past, the "win by two" rule produced very long sets and matches. Sets might be won by scores of 8-6, 9-7, 10-8, and so on. To make matches shorter, the tiebreak is often used when a set is tied at six games apiece. The rules for the tiebreak are special. Each player gets several chances to serve. The first player to score seven points wins the tiebreak and the set. If the score in the tiebreak reaches 6-6, the play continues until, with the score even (deuce), one player scores two straight points.

The 6-7(6) score in the first set means that at six games apiece, Nadal and Puerta played a tiebreak. The score in the tiebreak was tied at 6-6 until Puerta finally won the game. Puerta won this first set. But Nadal won the championship match, three sets to one.

Rafa was thrilled. "I am very happy," he said after the match. "Is a dream for me. I ... won today against the number one — not only against the number one for the tennis, but the number one for the person."

ALL IN THE FAMILY

Rafael Nadal Parera was born June 3, 1986, in the town of Manacor. It is on Mallorca, an island in the Mediterranean Sea. Many members of the Nadal family still live in one house in Manacor. On the ground floor are Rafa's grandparents. One flight up live his Uncle Toni, Toni's wife, and their three daughters. On the floor above them are Rafa's parents, Sebastián (who is a businessman) and Ana María. Above them, on the top floor, lives Rafa's younger sister, María Isabel, or Maribel. Rafa's own room is also on the top floor. He stays there when he's not living out of a suitcase on the men's pro tour.

Tough Competitors

Sports skills run in Rafa's family. His uncle, Toni Nadal, is his tennis coach. Another uncle, Miguel Angel Nadal,

Island Sports

The island of Mallorca (mah-YOR-kah) belongs to Spain. The name is also spelled Majorca. Farms here grow olives, almonds, fruits, and grains. Tourism is also a big source of income. About 35,000 people live in Manacor, the Nadal family's hometown.

Many visitors come to Mallorca for the fishing. Diving, windsurfing, and waterskiing are popular. The island is also a center for horseback riding, cycling, tennis, and golf.

Rafa gets a hug from his uncle and coach, Toni Nadal, after his first Grand Slam victory.

is a famous soccer player. He played on Spain's soccer team, which competed for the World Cup.

Rafa's uncles didn't go easy on him. When he lost to them at tennis or soccer, they would mock him by calling him "champion." Rafa took it hard. "When they beat him, it would bother him so much," says his father. "He couldn't tolerate it. He would become sick."

A Part-time Lefty

Rafa was only about four years old when he got his first tennis racket. He was a natural right-hander. But after Rafa had been playing for a while, Uncle Toni had a bright idea. He thought Rafa might be a better tennis player if he held the racket with his left hand. The experiment worked brilliantly — but only for Rafa's tennis game. "Apart from the tennis," says Rafa,

FACT FILE

For years, Miguel Angel Nadal played for a soccer club in Barcelona, a large city in Spain. He got the nickname "Beast of Barcelona" because of his very tough defense.

Game of Love

In tennis, the word "love" has a special meaning. It stands for zero. A server who wins the first point in a game, for example, takes the lead by 15-0, or "fifteen-love." If the server loses the first point, the score is 0-15, or "love-fifteen." A player who wins a set by 6-0 is said to have won "six-love."

How did love come to mean zero? Some tennis writers think it began with the French word *l'oeuf*. This word sounds like "love" and means "the egg." It's easy to see that an egg has a shape like a zero. The same idea can be seen in the English term "goose egg," which means a big, fat zero!

Nadal can race from one side of the court to the other, hitting balls many players wouldn't even try to return.

13

"I can do nothing with my left hand. I eat, write, and all other things I do with my right hand."

A reporter once asked Nadal what he would be if he hadn't become a tennis player. A soccer player, Rafa answered. Uncle Toni agrees. He notes that until Rafa was twelve, he played more soccer than tennis. "If it weren't for tennis, Rafa would probably be a soccer star right now," he says. "That's how good an athlete he is."

FACT FILE

Many tennis champions have been left-handed. Lefties include such all-time greats as Jimmy Connors, John McEnroe, and Martina Navratilova. Nadal is the best left-handed player in tennis today.

RISING STAR

CHAPTER 3

Success in
tennis came quickly to the
young Nadal. By the time
he was twelve, he had
won several youth
championships. In
2000, he finished first in the
"fourteen and under" class at the
European Junior Masters event.

Uncle Toni remained his coach.
But Rafa also began practicing with
Spanish tennis star Carlos Moya. Nadal
praises Moya as both a good friend and
a great guy. "An example to follow," Rafa
says. "He's modest, friendly, and has
helped me a lot."

FACT FILE

Like Nadal, Carlos Moya was born on Mallorca. He
turned pro in 1995. During his first ten years on the
pro tennis tour, Moya won more than $11 million.

Going Pro

Nadal joined the men's pro tour when he was only fifteen. His mother wasn't wild about his decision. She wanted him to stay in school. "I took it very badly," she admits. "I could not consent to him not studying. But life keeps on imposing things on you. Besides, among the people that he's with, no one studies. ... He lives his own life." In 2001 and 2002, he played mostly Futures matches against other young players. He won six Futures titles in 2002. Most of his victories were on clay courts in Spain.

Wimbledon Breakthrough

Nadal branched out in 2003. He played matches in many major cities in Europe, testing himself against the top-ranked pros. At a tournament in Hamburg, Germany, he beat his friend Moya. At the time, Moya was ranked fifth in the world.

FACT FILE

In some ways, Nadal is similar to Boris Becker, a German tennis star who achieved great success as a teenager. Becker holds the record as the youngest man ever to win Wimbledon (seventeen years, seven months). He won Wimbledon singles titles in 1985, 1986, and 1989.

"Beaten by a Child"

Pat Cash, an Australian tennis champ, was quick to see Nadal's talent. On a visit to Mallorca in 2001, he agreed to play a match against the local favorite. Cash was in his mid-thirties. He thought the fourteen-year-old Rafa still looked like a child. He was embarrassed when the teenage boy beat him.

Four years later, Cash shared his memories with the *London Sunday Times*. "Nadal came bounding out like this was his big chance. ... Fist pumps, posturing, shouted celebrations. If I heard the yell *vamos* ['let's go!'] once, I heard it 100 times."

Cash took the first set. Nadal won the second. They played a tiebreak to decide the match. "He had been sending the most amazing winners flying past my racket. ... [In the tiebreak] there he was at the net, diving to make seemingly impossible volleys. ... Once I got over my initial anger at being beaten by a child, I realized I had just encountered a talent that could win tennis's greatest prizes."

One of the first tennis stars to recognize Rafa's potential was Pat Cash, a Wimbledon winner in his younger years.

In June, at the age of seventeen, Rafa played Wimbledon for the first time. It was his first Grand Slam event. He won his first two matches but was knocked out in the third round. He was the youngest player on the men's tour to reach the third round at Wimbledon since Boris Becker in 1984. Like Becker, he won fans by diving for difficult shots.

In September, Nadal made his first trip to the U.S. Open. He lost in the second round but proved he could stand up to Grand Slam pressure. At the end of the 2002 tour, he was ranked 235th. By the close of the 2003 season, he was 66th. The Spanish sensation was on his way.

Nadal and Carlos Moya are friends both on and off the court. The two were team-mates on the Spanish team that won the Davis Cup in 2004.

THE SPANISH ARMADA

More than four hundred years ago, King Philip II of Spain built a huge navy. It was called the Spanish Armada. In 1588, the king ordered his fleet to strike England. The English navy was smaller, but it had help from the weather. Strong winds blew the Armada off course, and the English were able to attack it. The Armada sailed back to Spain in tatters.

In 2004, Spain put together a more successful Armada. This one struck with tennis rackets instead of ships. Its aim was not to invade England but to win the Davis Cup, a series of matches in which teams from different countries compete. Unlike King Philip's navy, this new Armada won its battles. Leading the charge was Spain's youngest tennis warrior, Rafael Nadal.

A Troubled Summer

Rafa started well in 2004. He began winning consistently on hard courts as well as clay. In January, he reached the finals at a tournament in New Zealand. In March, he beat Federer in Miami. But then Rafa hurt his ankle. He was out for three months and missed the French Open and Wimbledon. At the U.S. Open in late summer, Rafa was outclassed by Andy Roddick. The American won in three sets, 6-0, 6-3, 6-4.

Nadal did not expect to start in the Davis Cup Final. One spot on the Spanish team went to his friend, Carlos Moya. A second slot was reserved for another big gun, Juan Carlos Ferrero. But Ferrero got hurt, and Rafa became a last-minute replacement. His job was to beat Roddick in a singles match on the first day of play.

FACT FILE

Juan Carlos Ferrero had his best year in 2003. That year, he won the French Open. Later, he reached the U.S. Open final, losing to Roddick. Ferrero has won more than $10 million in his pro career.

The Davis Cup

On the pro tour, players compete in singles matches as individuals. When they win, they win for themselves. The Davis Cup is different. For the Davis Cup, men compete as members of their country's team. When they win, they win for their country.

Countries have taken part in Davis Cup play for more than a hundred years. Teams in various regions of the world compete to join the World Group, which is made up of sixteen countries. These countries play matches against each other. The Davis Cup Final is usually held in a different country each year. It takes place in late November or early December.

Each Davis Cup match lasts three days. On the first day, each team's number-one player faces the other team's number-two player. On the second day, the teams play a doubles match. On the final day, the number ones play each other. Then, the number twos play their own match. The winning team must take three of the five matches.

For many years, the Davis Cup was played for a trophy and national honor. In 1981, cash prizes were introduced. Prize money in 2005 totaled $8.5 million.

Rafa shakes hands with Andy Roddick after beating him in a key Davis Cup singles match.

Capturing the Cup

Rafa had an edge over Roddick, who played for the U.S. team. His ankle injury had healed. He was playing in his home country, Spain, on a red clay court in Sevilla. The stadium was filled with more than 27,000 screaming fans. The noise of the home crowd helped to pump up Rafa. "It was crazy," says Roddick. "It was unlike anything I've experienced before."

The eighteen-year-old Rafa proved unbeatable. He kept Roddick off-balance by mixing powerful groundstrokes with tricky drop shots. He lost the first set but roared back to win the next three, 6-2, 7-6(6), 6-2. The only man ever to play (and win) a Davis Cup Final singles match at a younger age was Boris Becker, in 1985. "This has certainly been the match of my life," Nadal said later. "I think fifty percent of the victory is because of the fans."

FACT FILE

Sevilla (pronounced say-VEE-yah) is a sunny city in southern Spain. In English it is often spelled Seville and pronounced seh-VILL.

Mr. Muscles

It's hard to miss the muscles rippling beneath Nadal's shirt. "His biceps are bigger than my head," jokes the top-ranked U.S. player, Andy Roddick. Surprisingly, Rafa insists his bulging biceps don't come from the weight room. It's just the way he's built.

His Uncle Toni agrees. "The family is all strong people," he says. "Rafa ... he was always strong. At sixteen, his body just exploded."

"He can be intimidating," says Roddick's coach, Dean Goldfine. "Not the biceps but his running. He's going left, right, center, up and back. And after he gets the point he's jumping around, fresh as a daisy, while his opponent is taking his last gasp of air."

Powerfully built, Rafa hits his groundstrokes with tremendous force.

RAFA MANIA

The Nadal buzz grew louder and louder in the first half of 2005. In February, Rafa won clay-court tournaments in Brazil and Mexico. In March, he reached the final on the hard courts of Miami. Still only eighteen, he took a two-set lead against the mighty Federer. But he lost a tiebreak in the third set and faded in the last two.

During the spring, he won four straight tournaments on clay, including the French Open. In August, he outslugged Andre Agassi to win a hard-court tournament in Montreal, Canada.

There was almost as much buzz about Nadal's fashion choices as his racket skills. In 2005, Rafa sported bright shirts and calf-length white pants. He calls them his *piratas*, or pirate pants. They're also known as Capris. Stores sold hundreds

Nadal outhit and outran Andre Agassi to win his first major hard-court tournament in August 2005.

FACT FILE

Roger Federer was born in Switzerland in 1981. He turned pro in 1998. Federer has been the top-ranked player in men's tennis since early 2004. He has already won more than $19 million.

Name Brands and Dollar Signs

Pro tennis players make money by winning matches. They also make money by signing deals with big companies to use those companies' products. Nadal doesn't wear that Nike "swoosh" on his white headband just because he likes the design!

Rafa wears Nike clothes and Nike Air Max Breathe Free II tennis shoes. He swings a Babolat AeroPro Drive racket. He's very much aware of the brands he uses. In 2004, a reporter for a Spanish magazine asked to see his first tennis racket. "I would show it to you, but I can't," Rafa answered. "It's not Babolat."

James Blake was the crowd favorite when he upset Nadal at the 2005 U.S. Open. The American beat Rafa in four sets, 6-4, 4-6, 6-3, 6-1.

of them after Rafa started wearing them on the court. "He's really just a dreamboat for young girls," says the fashion editor of *Teen People* magazine.

Aiming to Improve

In the first ten months of 2005, Nadal earned more than $3.8 million. He won eleven titles on the men's pro tour, the most ever by a teenager. Federer also won eleven titles in the same period. The Swiss right-hander won two Grand Slam events, Wimbledon and the U.S. Open.

Nadal lost in the second round at Wimbledon. He had higher hopes for the U.S. Open. But he lost to an American, James Blake, in the third round. The match was hard for Nadal because Blake had the crowd with him the whole time. After the match, Rafa tried to be a good sport.

FACT FILE

In 2005, James Blake was making a comeback from a terrible year in 2004. First, he broke his neck when his head hit a net post. Then, his father died of cancer. Finally, Blake had a serious illness. It took him many months to recover.

Down by two sets against Ivan Ljubicic of Croatia, Rafa roared back to win his eleventh championship on the 2005 men's pro tour.

"I know James has had some difficult moments," he said. "And so I'm happy for him. I like to see people do well who have suffered and been through hard things."

Nadal would like to become more popular in the United States. To do so, he needs to improve his English. He would also like to become an excellent all-court player, like Federer.

Someday, Rafa says, he hopes to win Wimbledon and take his place among the great tennis champions. "I need to improve my volley. I need to improve my serve. I need to improve my confidence on grass. And for that I need to play a lot more matches. Wimbledon will be my goal until the day I retire."

TIME LINE

1986 Rafael Nadal Parera is born June 3 in Manacor, Mallorca.

1990 Begins playing tennis, with his uncle Toni as his coach.

2000 Wins in the "fourteen and under" class at the European Junior Masters tournament.

2001 Turns pro at the age of fifteen.

2002 In Futures events, he becomes a top player on the clay courts of Spain.

2003 At seventeen, he is the youngest player to reach the third round of the Wimbledon men's singles since Boris Becker in 1984.

2004 Leads Spain to a Davis Cup Final victory over the United States.

2005 Wins his first Grand Slam tournament, the French Open. In the men's pro tennis rankings, he rises from fifty-first place to second place.

GLOSSARY

deuce — in tennis, a game or set that is tied.

drop shots — shots that are hit softly, so they fall close to the net.

encountered — met, especially as an opponent.

Futures matches — tennis matches in which up-and-coming pros compete.

Grand Slam — in tennis, the four biggest pro tennis tournaments each year. They are the Australian Open, the French Open, Wimbledon, and the U.S. Open.

groundstrokes — shots that are hit after the ball bounces, usually from deep in the court.

love — in tennis, a score of zero.

rallies — exchanges of shots as a point is played.

serve — the shot that begins a point.

tiebreak — a game with special rules played when a set is tied at six games apiece.

topspin — the way a tennis ball moves when the racket hits the back of the ball with a sharp upward stroke.

tournament — a series of games or contests.

volleys — returns that are hit before the ball takes a bounce.

TO FIND OUT MORE

BOOKS

Getting into Tennis. Ron Thomas and Joe Herran.
   (Chelsea House)

How to Play Tennis. Venus and Serena Williams
   (DK Publishing)

Tennis. History of Sports (series). Victoria Sherrow
   (Lucent)

VIDEOS

Coach: Making Grand Slam Champions (Msl Music) NR

The Wimbledon Video Collection: The 2005 Official Film
   (Kultur) NR

WEB SITES

ATPtennis.com
www.atptennis.com/en/
The official site for men's pro tennis

Roland-Garros
www.fft.fr/rolandgarros/en/Frame_RG.html
Useful information about the French Open

VamosRafael.com
www.vamosrafael.com/home.html
A first-rate fan site

INDEX

About the Author

Geoffrey M. Horn has been a fan of music, movies, and sports for as long as he can remember. He has written more than two dozen books for young people and adults, along with hundreds of articles for encyclopedias and other works. He lives in southwestern Virginia, in the foothills of the Blue Ridge Mountains, with his wife, their collie, and four cats. He dedicates this book to the memory of Bud Skeens.

SUPER DC HEROES

SUPERMAN

LIVEWIRE!

WRITTEN BY
BLAKE A. HOENA

ILLUSTRATED BY
DAN SCHOENING

SUPERMAN CREATED BY
JERRY SIEGEL AND
JOE SHUSTER

Stone Arch Books
MINNEAPOLIS   SAN DIEGO

EASY
SUPERMAN

Published by Stone Arch Books in 2010
151 Good Counsel Drive, P.O. Box 669
Mankato, Minnesota 56002
www.stonearchbooks.com

Library of Congress Cataloging-in-Publication Data

Hoena, B. A.
  Livewire! / by Blake A. Hoena ; illustrated by Dan Schoening.
    p. cm. -- (DC super heroes. Superman)
  ISBN 978-1-4342-1566-6 (lib. bdg.) -- ISBN 978-1-4342-1733-2 (pbk.)
  [1. Superheroes--Fiction.] I. Schoening, Dan, ill. II. Title.
  PZ7.H67127Li 2010
  [Fic]--dc22

                                        2009008739

Summary: During a rock concert, a bolt of lightning strikes Metropolis shock
jock Leslie Willis. When she awakes, Willis has gained the power to control
electricity . . . and gained an even greater anger toward Superman. Soon, the
newly named Livewire sends shockwaves throughout the city and threatens
the lives of Metropolis' citizens. Only Superman can stop this deadly Electric
Lady.

Art Director: Bob Lentz
Designer: Bob Lentz

Printed in the United States of America

TABLE OF CONTENTS

CHAPTER 1

SHOCK JOCK

At Stryker's Island Prison, a guard patrolled a long hallway. His boots clicked loudly on the concrete floor, and his footsteps echoed down the corridor.

The hall was lined with cells designed to hold Metropolis' most dangerous criminals. The guard paused in front of each cell, making sure the criminal it imprisoned was safely inside. One of them held Rudy Jones, also known as the villainous Parasite. He could suck the energy from living things just by touching them.

Rudy was sitting on his bunk as the guard stopped in front of his cell. He looked up and asked, "What time is it?"

"Almost 9:00 a.m.," the guard replied.

"Time for the *Livewire* show," Rudy said.

"I know," the guard said. "I'll turn on the radio as soon as I get back to my desk."

"Thanks," Rudy said.

The guard turned away from Rudy and continued down the corridor. At the end of the hallway sat a desk with a small radio on it. The guard plopped down in a chair and turned on the radio. A female voice squealed across the airwaves.

"Wake up, Metropolis! This is WLXL, 95.5 Alive. It's time for *Livewire*, the only show you should have your twitchy little ears tuned to. I'm your host Leslie Willis."

Down the hallway, Rudy sat in his bunk, smiling. He leaned forward to listen closer to what Leslie had to say.

"Turn it up," Rudy said.

The guard leaned across the desk, turning the volume knob on the radio.

"Today, I'd like to talk about one of my least favorite topics: Superman," shrieked the shock jock. "Is Superman really a hero? Or is he just a caped Boy Scout telling all the baddies where Metropolis is?

"Sure, he may have stopped Brainiac from destroying Earth. But think about it, people. How many of you ever heard of Brainiac before Superman came along? Or Metallo? Or Bizarro for that matter?

"Dare I say it?

"Not one of you!"

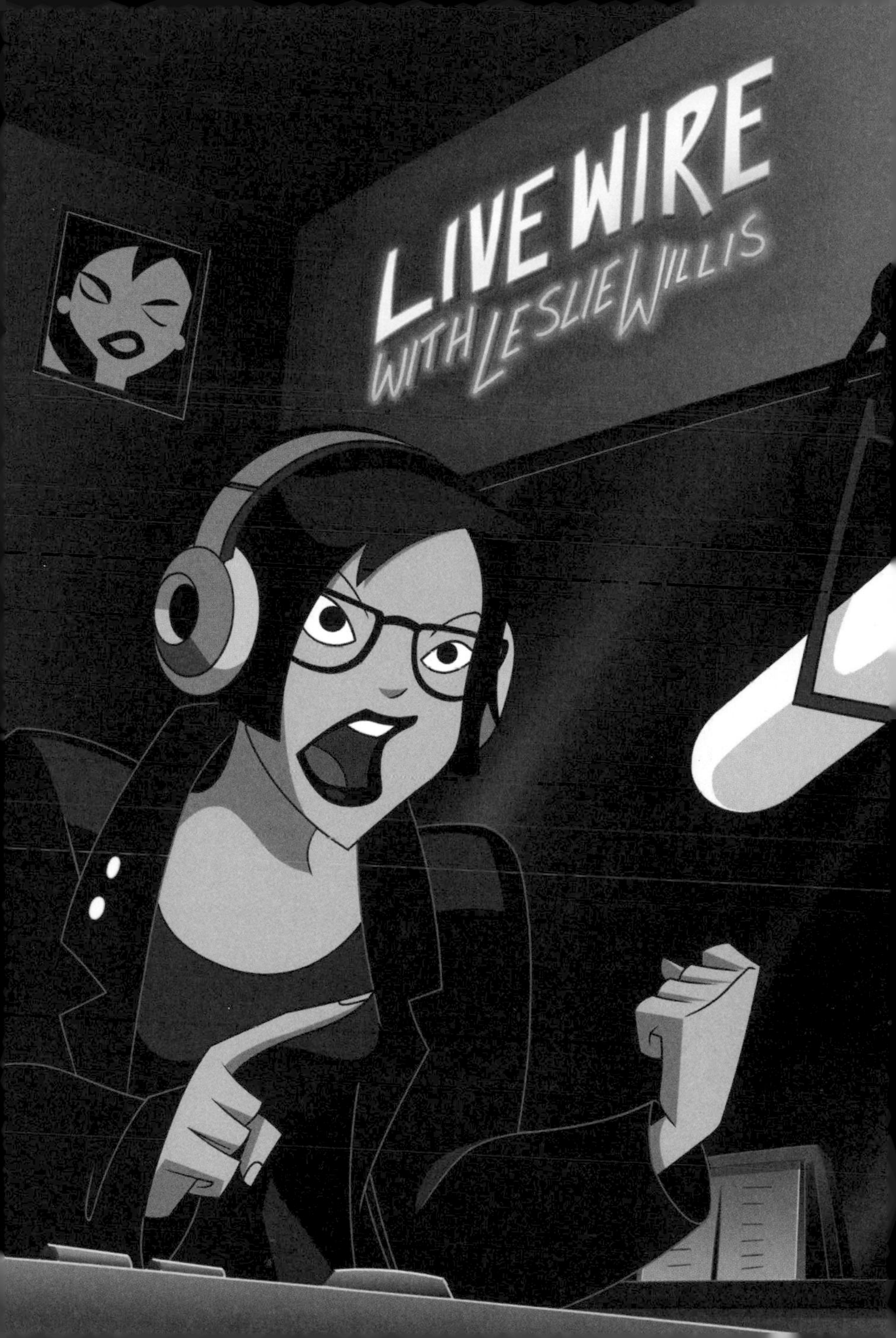
LIVE WIRE
WITH LESLIE WILLIS

"She's got a point," said Jimmy Olsen. The youthful photographer for the *Daily Planet* sat in the paper's newsroom with reporters Lois Lane and Clark Kent. They were listening to Leslie on the radio.

"Jimmy," Lois scolded. "Superman has saved your life and mine several times."

"I mean, uh, I just," Jimmy stumbled over his words, embarrassed. "Just because I listen to Willis's show doesn't mean I don't like Superman."

"Hmf!" Lois folded her arms across her chest in dismay. She added, "I can't believe people listen to this garbage. She's just saying bad things about Superman to increase her ratings."

"Quiet," Clark said. "I want to hear what else she has to say."

". . . Superman is a trouble magnet," Leslie continued. "If that super jerk wasn't polluting our skies, super-villains wouldn't give a hoot about Metropolis. For all my fans who feel the same, come down to Centennial Park tonight. I'm having a big party. We're going to celebrate my three-year dominance of the airwaves!"

Just then, Perry White, editor-in-chief of the *Daily Planet*, entered the newsroom.

"I'm glad you're such big fans of Miss Willis," Perry said. "Because I'm sending you down to Centennial Park tonight."

"But, Perry," Lois said. "Did you hear what she said about —"

"I don't care!" Perry cut her off. "This celebration will be a huge event. I want my best reporters there."

Looking at Jimmy, Perry added, "And you can take some photographs."

"Great!" Jimmy exclaimed. "Maybe I can get Leslie's autograph."

There was a long pause as everyone glared at Jimmy.

"What?" Jimmy asked. "She's popular with all the kids."

Suddenly, Perry shouted, "What're you all sitting around for? We've got a paper to run!"

CHAPTER 2

A REAL SHOCKER

Later that night, at Centennial Park, Clark and Jimmy stood at the back of a large crowd. In front of them was a stage covered with lights and thumping speakers. On stage, a band played, with guitars wailing and drums pounding.

"I won't get Leslie's autograph from back here," Jimmy shouted over the noise.

Clark frowned at him.

"I mean," Jimmy said with a grin, "I won't get any good pictures."

"I think I saw Lois up near the stage," Clark said. "Why don't you go find her?"

Jimmy shoved his way into the wall of people and quickly disappeared. Clark stayed back, keeping his eye on things. On the ground, the crowd cheered and screamed. Flickers of lightning danced among the black clouds above.

Glancing at his watch, Clark noticed that a few raindrops had dampened his sleeve. *Looks like Mother Nature isn't one of Leslie's fans,* Clark thought.

Up on stage, the band ended their song, and the crowd cheered. **RUMMMMMMMBLE!** A deep, thunderous sound mixed with the applause. More rain fell, and more lightning flashed. The crowd kept cheering as the ground turned to mud beneath their feet.

Before the band could begin another song, a police officer stepped onto the stage. He walked up to the microphone.

"Sorry, folks," the police officer said. "There's a severe thunderstorm headed our way. We ask that everyone seek shelter. It's for your own safety. I'm afraid the show is canceled."

Just then, Leslie walked onto the stage. Her dark eyes and darker hair were nearly as black as the overcoat she wore. She snatched the microphone from the police officer.

"It appears we have a problem, people!" Leslie shouted as she stomped around on the stage. "The cops want to shut the party down. What do you say to that?"

"Booooooo!" the crowd roared.

"Are you gonna let them tell us what to do?" she asked.

"No!" the crowd screamed.

Turning toward the police officer, Leslie said, "See, what we have here is a democracy. And the people have spoken!"

Leslie held the microphone out to the crowd. "LESLIE! LESLIE! LESLIE!" they chanted wildly.

Seeing that things were turning ugly, Clark ducked into an alley. With no one around, he quickly shedded his suit and tie to reveal his true identity. He was Superman, Last Son of Krypton. The rays from Earth's yellow sun gave him unimaginable powers. Superman leaped into the air and flew above the swarm of people. He zoomed toward the stage.

Meanwhile, the scene continued to grow uglier. The clouds darkened overhead, and lightning crackled in the background. People screamed and hollered as Leslie riled them up.

"Come on! Say it with me, people," Leslie yelled as the wind whipped her hair around. "We're not gonna take it!"

"We're not gonna take it!" the crowd echoed. "WE'RE NOT GONNA TAKE IT!"

When Superman landed on the stage, the masses quieted. But Leslie quickly turned on him.

"Look here, people!" Leslie sneered. "The cops brought a man in a cape."

The crowd roared with laughter.

"You're endangering these people," Superman whispered to Leslie.

"Did you hear that?" Leslie yelled to the crowd. "Ol' big blue's got his PJs on. He needs his beauty rest and wants everyone else to go to bed like good little boys and girls," Leslie ranted.

"What do you say to that?" Leslie asked the swarm of people.

The crowd jeered. The shock jock had turned her fans against the Man of Steel. Now they all acted just like her.

KA-BOOM! Overhead, lightning flashed. Thunder boomed.

BZZT! The microphone in Leslie's hand crackled. Buckets of rain fell, soaking everyone. Gusts of wind tore at people's clothes. Worried faces poked up in the crowd as the weather worsened, but Leslie would not stop.

"See, Superman," she screeched. "I'm the ringmaster of this circus. People listen to me. Not the TV. Not the papers. Not some muscle-bound creep in tights!"

As if on cue, lightning struck the top of the stage. **ZZZAPPPPPPPP!**

Lights flickered. Speakers popped. Electricity crackled everywhere.

Superman leaped in front of the lightning as it shot onto the stage. He tried to shield Leslie. Electric fingers sizzled and snapped, wrapping Superman in pale blue light.

"Arrgh!" Superman groaned in pain.

Leslie stumbled backwards, away from Superman. But she wasn't quick enough. The lightning jumped from Superman to her. She was caught in its crackling grasp.

 Leslie screamed.

Sparks covered her body. Her hair stood on end. Bolts of electricity shot out of her eyes, her fingers, and her toes. She cried out in agony.

Then she collapsed.

The party was over.

CHAPTER 3

LIVEWIRE

The next day, at Metropolis General Hospital, Leslie woke up. She was lying in bed and wearing a hospital gown.

She didn't feel any pain. But she was shocked by what she saw. "What happened to me?" she shrieked, looking down at her hands.

Leslie quickly jumped out of the hospital bed. She ran over to a mirror. Her skin was chalky white. Her black hair had turned pale blue.

"Superman!" Leslie screeched. "This is all his fault!"

THUD! THUD! Leslie pounded on the wall with her fists.

"Oooohhhhh!" she growled in anger.

KRAK! The air around Leslie came to life. It crackled with white flashes of energy. Suddenly, the TV in her room snapped on. Its screen showed an image of last night's celebration. Dark clouds loomed over a cheering crowd.

"During their confrontation," a newscaster reported, "Superman and Leslie Willis were both struck by lightning. Superman was unharmed. But Metropolis' favorite shock jock is still in the hospital."

"Wait until I get my hands on Superman!" Leslie snarled.

Angrily, Leslie held out her hands in front of her, as if she were strangling someone. Blue bolts of electricity crackled between her fingers.

"Hey, what's this?" Leslie asked, surprised. "Hmmm. Let me try something. I'm feeling a little power hungry."

She held her arms out and scrunched her face in concentration. **FzzT!** Bolts of energy leaped from the lights and the TV, encircling Leslie. They whirled about the room, crackling and sizzling. The air was alive with electricity.

"Ooh, that feels better!" Leslie laughed.

Just then, a nurse poked his head into the room. "What's going on in here?" he asked.

"Ever hear of knocking?" Leslie snapped.

She pointed a finger at the cowering nurse. A blast of energy erupted from Leslie's hand. *BZZT!* The bolt struck the nurse. He was thrown backwards and crashed to the floor.

Seconds later, two orderlies came into the room. Leslie threw bolts of electricity at them as well. They ducked out of the way. The lightning flashed past, leaving black, smoldering scars on the wall behind them.

"Okay, kids. I'm tired of playing with you," Leslie said, placing her hands on her hips. "I have bigger fish to fry."

One second, Leslie was standing in the middle of her hospital room. The next, she was a lightning bolt of dancing energy. Blue light flickered throughout the room as she streamed, crackling and sizzling, into one of the wall outlets. Then she was gone.

Metropolis was lit by thousands of neon lights. In the city's center, people hustled along the sidewalks. Cars beeped and honked in the streets. In the center of it all, mounted on the side of a tall building, was a huge TV screen. It flashed images of famous celebrities and clothing ads.

KA-BOOM! A bolt of lightning erupted from one of the street lamps. As the bolt faded, Leslie appeared in its place. Still dressed in her hospital gown, she looked around, admiring the scene.

"Ahhh, Metropolis," she said. "This is my kind of town. Lights. People. Energy!"

Leslie sneered. "Especially the energy."

Leslie lifted her hands above her head. Lights flickered and popped. Bolts of energy raced from them toward Leslie.

"Ha ha," Leslie laughed. "I'm getting a charge out of this!"

People screamed as flashes of electricity flew overhead, crashing into buildings. Shards of glass from shattered windows rained down as people ran for safety. Cars squealed their tires and raced away as chunks of concrete fell from buildings and thudded to the ground.

Soon, the streets were empty and quiet. "Hey," Leslie smirked. "Where'd everybody go? I was about to treat them to some shocking news."

"Still endangering people, I see," a voice spoke from above Leslie.

"Superman!" Leslie said with a gasp.

"I'm glad to see you're feeling better," Superman said.

"Actually, I'm feeling quite energized," Leslie replied. She pointed a finger at Superman. A blast of energy erupted from her hand, zapping him in the chest.

"Oof!" Superman grunted as he smashed into a building. Then he fell to the ground with a thud.

"You're not ruining *this* celebration, Superman," Leslie snickered. She whirled about in a flash of crackling light. Her hospital gown shimmered. Then it changed into a sleek black outfit. "And look, I even have a new party dress for the occasion!"

"Kinda neat, huh? I did that by electrifying the air around me," Leslie explained. "I'm pure energy now, baby!"

Superman stood up and walked over to Leslie. "Listen, Miss Willis," he began.

"Oh, and it's not Miss Willis anymore," she chuckled. She looked up at a billboard advertising her *Livewire* program. "My name is Livewire!"

"I'm just here to help," Superman said.

"I got enough help from you last night," Livewire said.

She aimed a blast of electricity at Superman. He dodged the bolt and then rushed toward her. But she was too quick. She changed into a bolt of energy. Livewire leaped into the TV overlooking the square. Suddenly, her face appeared on the screen.

"Ha, missed me, Superman! Now — lights out," Leslie laughed. "I hope you aren't afraid of the dark."

Everywhere, lights and TVs began to flicker. Then everything went dark.

CHAPTER 4

QUEEN OF ALL MEDIA

Back at the Daily Planet Building, Lois and Jimmy sat in the dark. There was no power. A candle sputtered on Lois's desk. It gave them just enough light to work by.

Mr. White approached them. He carried a typewriter. "Ah," Mr. White began. "This reminds me of the good old days — back before computers and the Internet were around."

"You mean," Jimmy said, making a face at the typewriter, "back when dinosaurs roamed the Earth?"

"Just because the power's out," Perry said, angrily, "doesn't mean we aren't going to put out a paper. Now get to work, you two!"

THUD! Perry slammed the typewriter down on Lois's desk. "And where's Clark?!" he asked. Suddenly all of the TVs and computers throughout Metropolis snapped on. Livewire's face appeared on all of the screens.

"Good evening, citizens of Metropolis!" Livewire squealed. "This is Livewire, coming to you at a gazillion megahertz. I've restored power to all your favorite media outlets. Now you can tune in to me, queen of all media!"

"Man, I am so sick of her," Jimmy said.

He reached over to turn off the radio.

As he did, an electric hand reached out of the radio and slapped him. **KRAK!**

"Ouch!" Jimmy yelped.

"Don't touch that dial, Metropolis," Livewire warned. "You are now my captive audience for the rest of your miserable lives!"

Miles away, in the control room of Metropolis' main power plant, Superman talked to the plant's foreman.

"I don't understand it, Superman," the foreman said. "The power is getting drained from the plant as fast as we can supply it."

"That's because there's a live wire on the other end," Superman said. "Can you shut the plant down?"

"Sure," the foreman replied, flipping switches. "It shouldn't take very long."

Throughout the power plant, machines huffed and clunked. Then the whir of the plant's generators suddenly began to grow quieter.

Downtown, on the big-screen TV, Livewire's face shined brightly.

"Okay, people," Livewire explained to the crowd gathered in the main square. "If you want your puny little lives to go back to normal, send me your money. All of it. Every last cent in your kiddies' piggy banks, too. From now on, I'm the media. I'm the electric company. I'm the telev —"

On the screen, Livewire's image flickered and crackled. TVs and computers in the city went blank. Radios were silent.

From downtown, a large spark emerged on a power line. It sizzled and popped, speeding toward the city's main power plant.

At the power plant, the spark leaped from the power line and transformed into Livewire. She looked into the plant's control room and saw Superman.

"Oh, that super jerk!" she gasped. "I should have known!"

BZZT! Livewire sent a bolt of electricity toward Superman. It hit him in the back. He was sent tumbling through one of the control room's windows. Livewire zapped over to the fallen hero as plant workers scrambled for their lives.

"Must you continue to rain on my parade?" she growled.

"Sorry, Miss Willis," Superman groaned. "But this power plant is offline. You won't get any more energy here."

"I've told you before. It's not Miss Willis, it's Livewire!" she screamed.

In the blink of an eye, Leslie turned into a bolt of energy. She leaped into a nearby power line. A spark of electricity zoomed along the line and quickly disappeared.

Superman turned to the plant's foreman. "Where's the nearest source of electricity?" he asked.

"The hydroelectric plant," the nervous foreman replied. "At the dam."

Superman flew away in a flash.

CHAPTER 5

FIZZLED OUT

A large spark sizzled along a power line. It raced toward Metropolis's hydroelectric plant. Once it reached the dam, the spark entered the plant's control room. Then it leaped from the wire, landing between some workers. As the spark faded, Livewire appeared in its place. The workers screamed and ran away.

"What? Never seen a girl before?" Livewire said, laughing.

Livewire lifted her hands. The plant's generators began to whir loudly.

"Time to recharge!" Livewire squealed.

FzzT! Bolts of energy leaped from the generators. They streamed through Livewire. Her body was illuminated in electric light.

"Ahhhh," she said. "That feels better."

High above, Superman sped toward the plant. He flew through its entrance and burst into the control room.

"You again!" Livewire growled. "You're becoming a pest."

Superman landed in front of Livewire. "Listen, Miss Willis," he began.

Livewire's face twisted in anger. She shot a blast of electricity at Superman. The bolt of energy slammed into his chest, sending him whirling across the room. Superman crashed into a wall and fell to the floor.

"It's Livewire!" she screeched. "Can't you get it through your thick skull?"

Superman groaned and struggled back to his feet.

"You want some more?" Livewire yelled.

BZZT! She sent another bolt of electricity at Superman. This time, he was prepared. He held his hands out in front of him, blocking the blast. As the bolt sizzled and snapped, Superman leaned into it. He pushed his way toward Livewire. Slowly, inch by inch, he crept closer as energy exploded from her fingers.

Once he was within reach, Superman leaped forward. He grabbed Livewire's hands. The pair struggled and then tumbled to the floor. They spun toward the control room's outer wall.

When they hit the outer wall, there was a loud blast. **BANG!** The wall cracked. Chunks of concrete thudded to the ground.

Superman and Livewire rolled outside. They didn't stop until they crashed into the foot of the dam.

With a burst of energy, Livewire tossed Superman aside.

"Get away from me!" Livewire yelled. She sent a bolt of electricity at Superman. It caught him in its grasp. He was tossed backward.

"I'm really getting tired of you," Livewire growled.

She sent bolt after bolt of electricity at Superman. As each one struck, he moaned in pain. **GROOOOAAAANNN!**

Livewire forced him backwards, until he was up against the wall of the dam.

"Now I've got you," Livewire chuckled. "And I promise, this is gonna hurt!"

A large ball of energy formed in Livewire's hand. It snapped and popped loudly as she threw it at Superman.

The ball raced toward Superman at lightning speed. But he was quicker. Superman ducked the blast. **BOOM!** It exploded against the dam's cement wall, creating a gaping hole.

FWOOSHHHHH!! A jet of water burst from the hole, striking Livewire. "Nooooo!" she screamed as water engulfed her.

Electricity crackled and sizzled all over Livewire's body. She screamed in pain.

The water was shorting her out. Then, with one final POP! the electricity in her body fizzled out. She collapsed and was carried away by the water.

With his heat vision, Superman quickly sealed the hole in the dam's wall. Once the water had stopped, he flew toward Livewire. He found her, passed out, near a shallow puddle of water.

47

Later that day, outside Livewire's jail cell, Superman talked with a prison guard.

"She's not going anywhere. Her cell is completely insulated," the guard explained. "Not even a spark can get in or out."

Superman looked into Livewire's cell through a thick plastic window. She slouched on her bunk. Her chin rested in the palms of her hands.

"I don't think the cell's big enough to contain her ego, though," Superman said.

The guard laughed nervously as the two of them turned from Livewire's cell and walked down the hallway.

Livewire jumped up from her bunk. She pounded on the window. **BANG! BANG!**

"Hey! Don't leave me in here alone," Leslie yelled.

"What am I going to do without an audience? Whom can I share my wisdom with?" Leslie pleaded.

In the cell across from her, Rudy Jones woke up.

"Hey, you're the lady from the radio," Rudy said. "I like what you have to say about Superman."

"Superman? Superman!" Leslie shrieked. "Why that caped Boy Scout! When I get my hands on him . . . "

FROM THE DESK OF CLARK KENT

WHO IS LIVEWIRE?

Leslie Willis was a radio show host known to electrify listeners with her controversial opinions. As Leslie began one of her anti-Superman rants at a live show, the Man of Steel came to warn her of an oncoming storm. As usual, she just mocked him. When lightning struck, Superman shielded Leslie as best he could, but the bolt passed through him and into her. Leslie was changed into a walking, talking spark plug — and she blames Superman for everything. As Livewire, she wants to use the Man of Steel as a lightning rod to get her revenge.

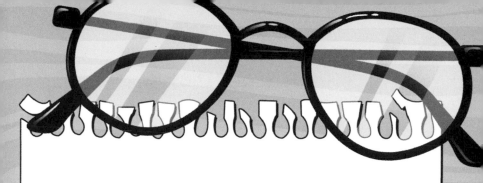

- Livewire possesses enough voltage to make her a difficult foe for the Man of Steel. Her power, while great, is not infinite — she must regularly recharge herself by sucking energy from Metropolis' power plants.

- As a radio shock jock, Leslie Willis ran wild on the airwaves of Metropolis radio. But as Livewire, she takes it a step further. She can **instantly ride the** airwaves — or the power lines — to anywhere in Metropolis!

- Superman seemed to have permanently short-circuited Livewire in a puddle of water. But Lex Luthor, Superman's arch-nemesis, brought the drained dynamo back to his secret lab and jolted her back to life!

- When Darkseid attacked Earth, Superman's heart stopped beating. Livewire realized that she, along with Earth itself, would be destroyed unless she revived the Man of Steel. So Livewire placed her hands on Superman's chest and gave his heart a shock, bringing him back to life and into the fight.

BIOGRAPHIES

Blake A. Hoena grew up in central Wisconsin, where, in his youth, he wrote stories about trolls lumbering around in the woods behind his parents' house. Later, he moved to Minnesota to pursue a Masters of Fine Arts degree in Creative Writing from Minnesota State University, Mankato. Since graduating, Blake has written more than thirty books for children. Most recently, he's working on a series of graphic novels about two space alien brothers, Eek and Ack, who are determined to conquer Earth.

Dan Schoening was born in Victoria, British Columbia, Canada. From an early age, Dan has had a passion for animation and comic books. Currently, Dan does freelance work in the animation and game industry and spends a lot of time with his lovely little daughter, Paige.

GLOSSARY

collapsed (kuh-LAPSD)—fell down suddenly from weakness

dampened (DAM-puhnd)—made something wet

dominance (DOM-uh-nuhnss)—to be the best at something, or the most powerful

emerged (i-MURJD)— became revealed or came into the open

engulfed (en-GUHLFD)—covered or swallowed up someone or something

generator (JEN-uh-ray-tur)—a machine that produces electricity by turning a magnet inside a coil of wire

hydroelectric (hye-droh-i-LEK-trik)—electricity produced by water power

insulated (IN-suh-late-id)—covered with a material that prevents electricity from escaping

restored (ri-STORD)—returned to normal

shattered (SHAT-urd)—broke into tiny pieces

villain (VIL-uhn)—an evil or wicked person

DISCUSSION QUESTIONS

1. Is Superman responsible for Livewire's change into a super-villain? Or is he innocent because he was trying to protect her?

2. Before she was struck by lightning, why do you think Livewire disliked Superman so much?

3. Leslie Willis expressed her opinions on her radio show no matter how controversial or dangerous they were. Do you think people should be able to say whatever they want or should some things be off-limits?

WRITING PROMPTS

1. Imagine that you can travel across power lines like Livewire. Where would you go? What would you do? Write about it.

2. Imagine that Livewire decided to be a super hero instead of a super-villain. Write about how she could help people using her electric powers.

3. Imagine that Livewire escapes from prison with the help of the power-stealing super-villain, Parasite. Write a short story about how they work together to break out of prison.

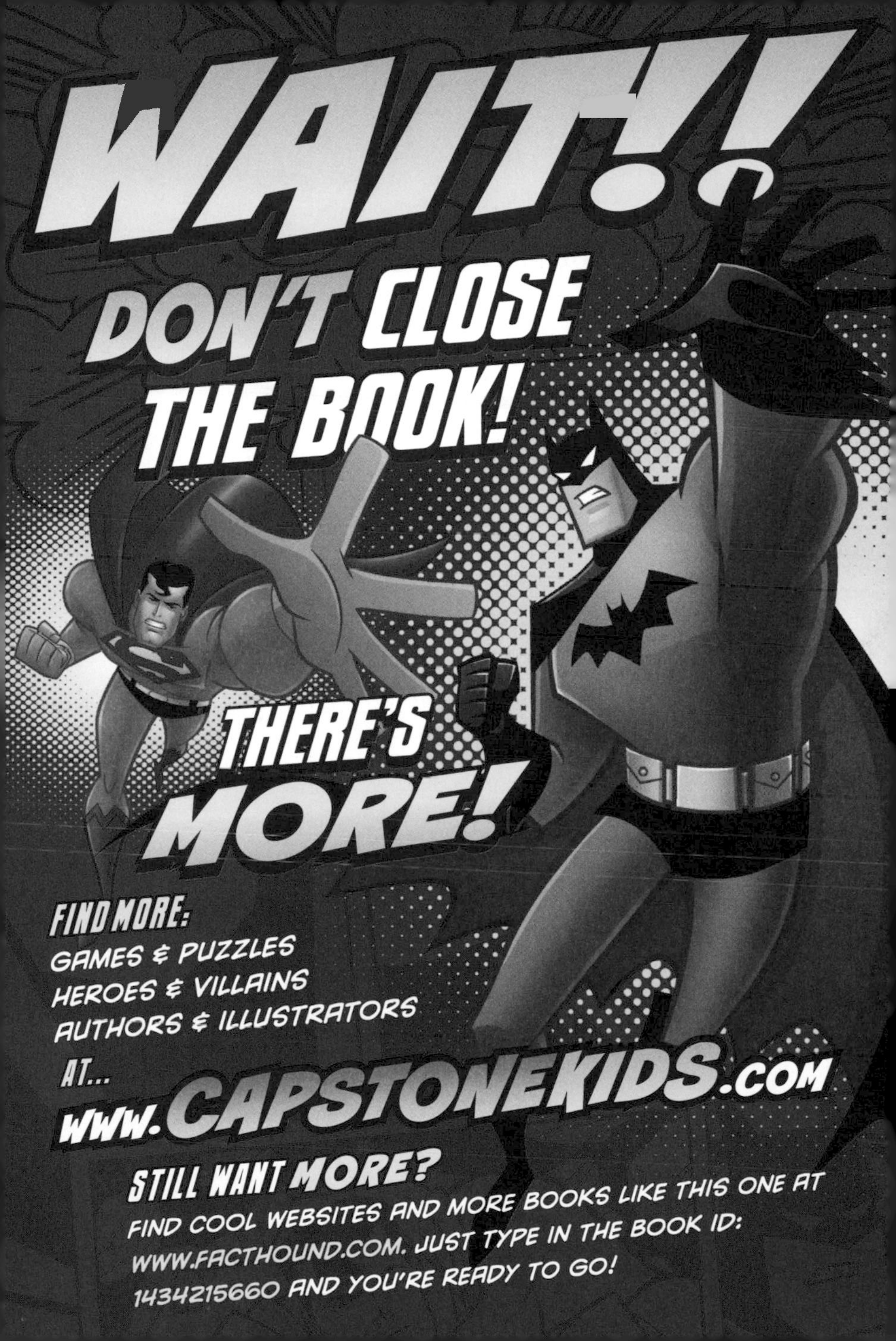
WAIT!!
DON'T CLOSE THE BOOK!
THERE'S MORE!
FIND MORE:
GAMES & PUZZLES
HEROES & VILLAINS
AUTHORS & ILLUSTRATORS
AT...
WWW.CAPSTONEKIDS.COM
STILL WANT MORE?
FIND COOL WEBSITES AND MORE BOOKS LIKE THIS ONE AT
WWW.FACTHOUND.COM. JUST TYPE IN THE BOOK ID:
1434215660 AND YOU'RE READY TO GO!

MORE NEW
SUPERMAN
ADVENTURES!

BIZARRO IS BORN!

METEOR OF DOOM

SUPER-VILLAIN
SHOWDOWN

THE KID WHO SAVED
SUPERMAN

THE SHRINKING CITY